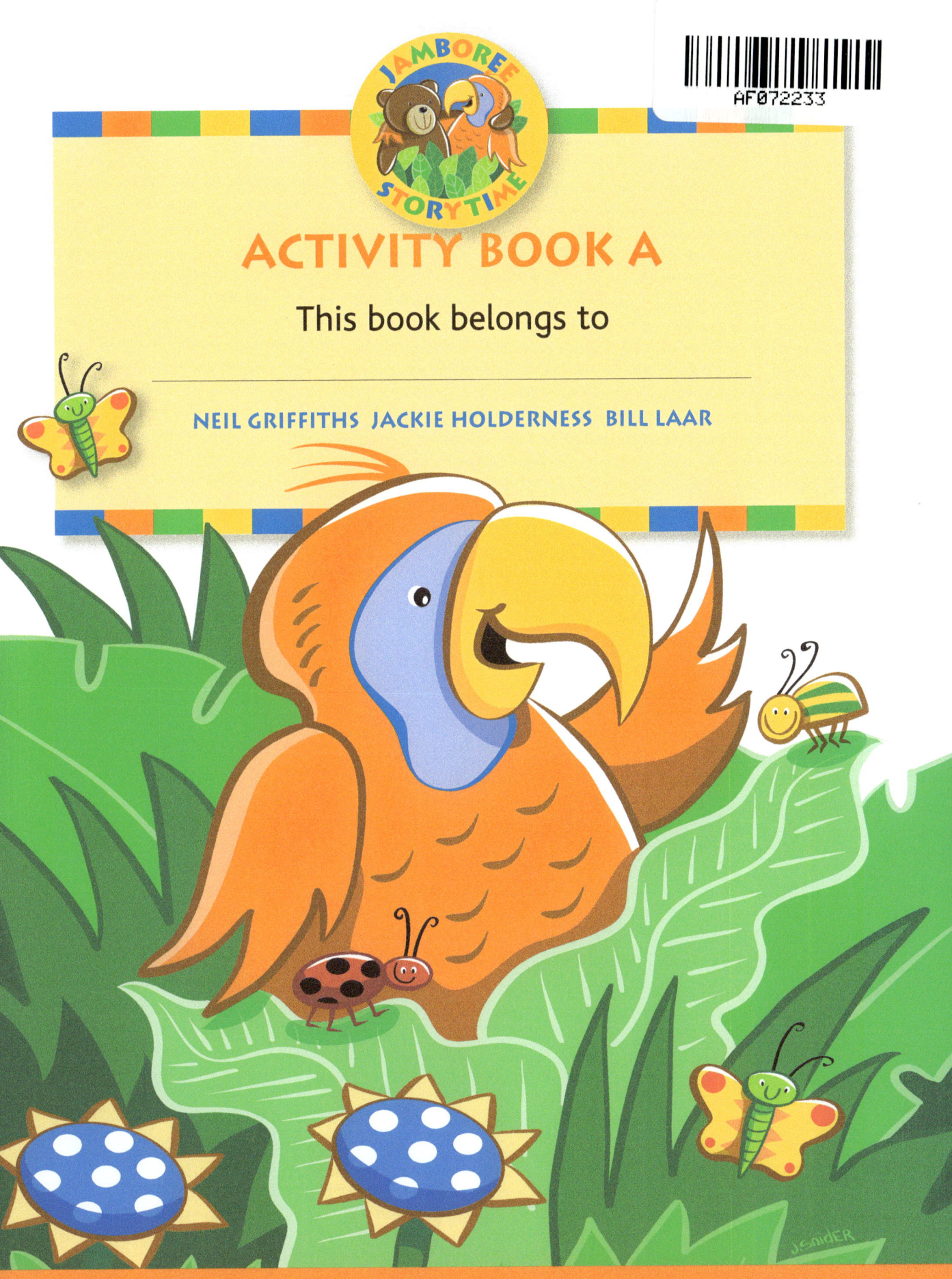

Published by Pearson Education Limited, Edinburgh Gate, Harlow, Essex, CM20 2JE.

Pearson Education Limited is a company incorporated in England and Wales, having its registered office at Edinburgh Gate, Harlow, Essex, CM20 2JE; Registered company number: 872828

© Jackie Holderness, Bill Laar, Neil Griffiths 2005

First published by Heinemann Educational Publishers in 2005
This edition published 2010

The moral right of the proprietor has been asserted.

All rights reserved. No part of this publication may be reproduced in any form or by any means (including photocopying or storing it in any medium by electronic means and whether or not transiently or incidentally to some other use of this publication) without the written permission of the copyright owner, except in accordance with the provisions of the Copyright, Designs and Patents Act 1988 or under the terms of a licence issued by the Copyright Licensing Agency, Saffron House, 6-10 Kirby Street, London EC1N 8TS (www.cla.co.uk). Applications for the copyright owner's written permission should be addressed to the publisher.

ISBN 9780435047214

ARP Impression 98

British Library Cataloguing in Publication Data
A full catalogue record for this book is available from the British Library.

Design by Jackie Hill @ 320 Design
Illustrated by Jackie Snider

Printed by Ashford Colour Press Ltd

> Guidance for using this Activity Book can be found in the *Jamboree Activity Guide*, free to download in the *Support materials* section of our website, www.pearsonglobalschools.com/jamboreestorytime

CONTENTS

5
Splash in the Ocean! Activities

17
Shark in the Park Activities

30
Five Little Ducks Activities

42
Baabooom! Activities

54
Kakadu Jack Activities

What colour?

 Join

A girl and a boy

 Draw

Fish swim home

 Match and join

Blowing bubbles

 Trace and draw

Fish pairs

  Cut out and match

Bingo!

  Listen and match

In the sea

  Colour

My friends

 Draw

Find five fish

  Look and circle

Spot the difference

  Look and circle

One, two, three, four, five

  Listen and join

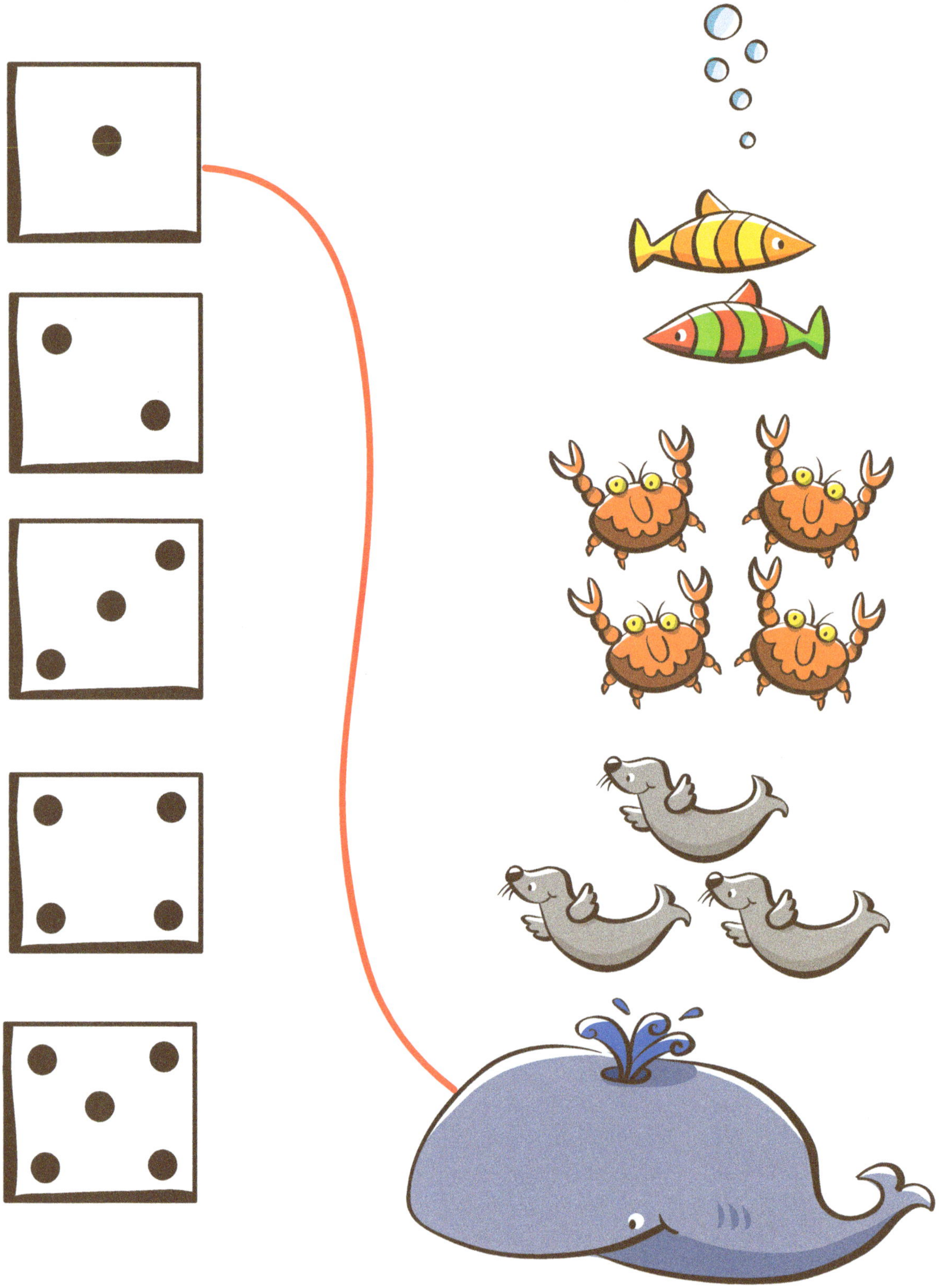

Find the telescope

 Colour

What is it?

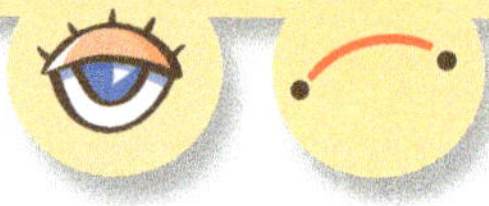

  Look and join

Find the cat

  Trace and join

Cats

 Look for cat pictures

Cat mask

 Cut

Patterns

  Trace and colour

My family

 Draw

How many?

 Count and join

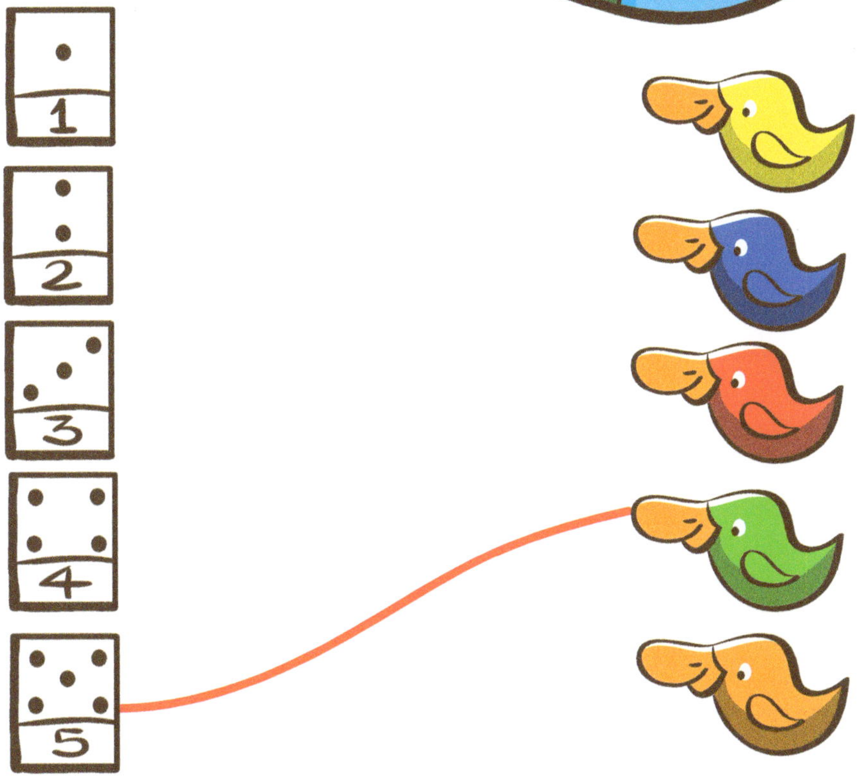

My hands

  Draw and colour

What is missing?

 Circle

T words

 Join

Colourful cats

  Listen and colour

Matching numbers

 Match and join

Big or little?

 Colour

Duck game

 Match and play

Spot the difference

 Point

Matching washing lines

  Draw and colour

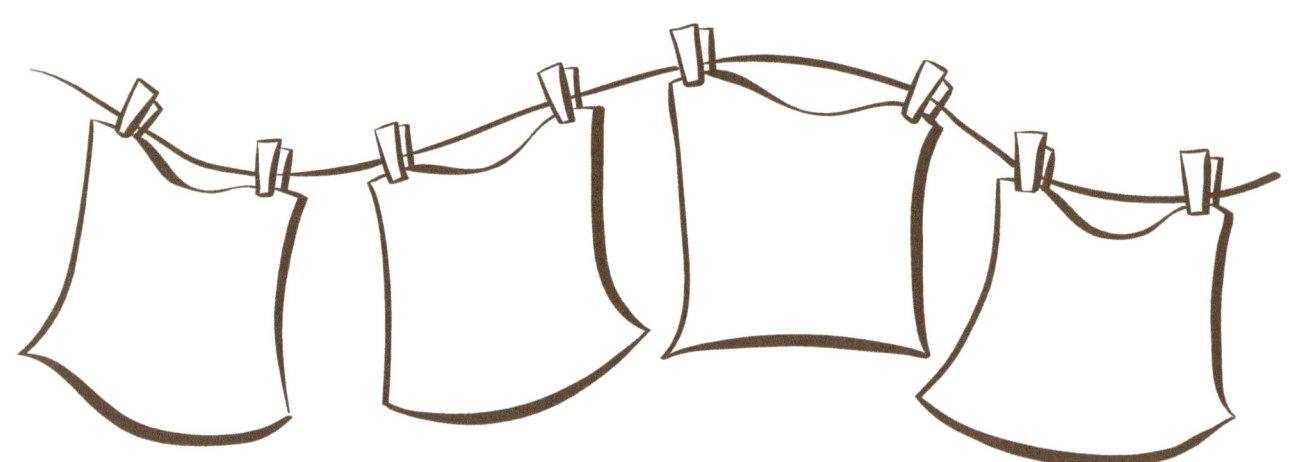

This is me!

 Draw

Find the hidden animals

 Point

Finish the butterfly

  Draw and colour

How many apples on each tree?

123 Count

Matching shoes

  Point and join

Lay the table bingo

 Match

Ducks, fish and dragonflies

  Count and colour

Red

 Colour

A red balloon

 Draw

The farmyard

  Colour

Small, medium, large

 Join

Who's in the farmyard?

  Look and circle

What colour is it?

   Colour and join

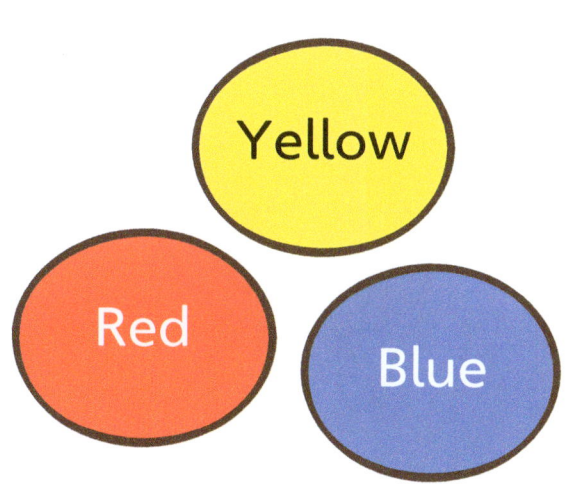

Animal fun

  Listen and colour

What's on the farm?

Cut

Give cow five spots

   Draw and colour

Who is it?

 Match

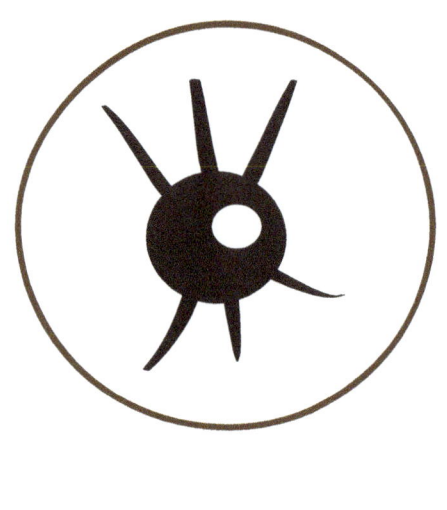

Floating away

 Draw

Find the sack and the sunshade

 Circle

Molly

 Colour

Mangoes, oranges and bananas

   Point and colour

Five fruits

  Colour and draw

Which fruit?

 Match

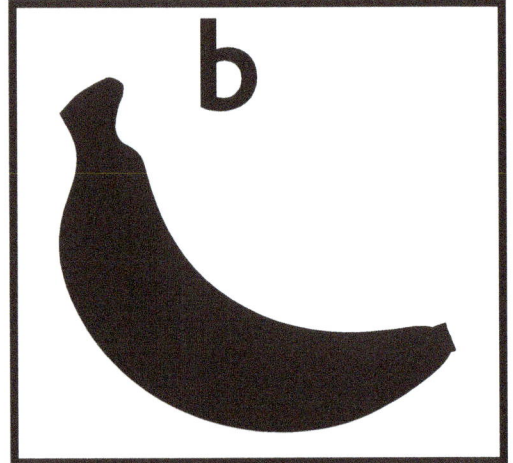

Find five bananas

 Circle

First, next, then

 Match

What is in the sack?

 Join

What did the parrot take?

  Look and circle

A sunshade and a parrot

   Join and colour

Molly's shopping

 Match

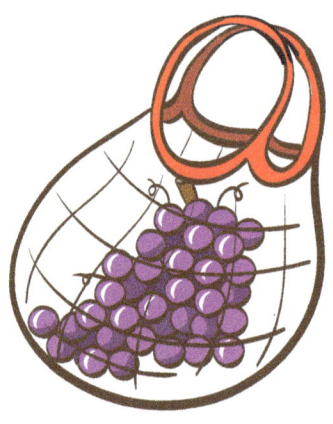

Put the fruit on the tables

 Match